Y0-CXN-280

LifeText

25 Lessons
Rarely
Taught in School

A book for children and adults

By Steven D. Cohn

Copyright © 2007 by Steven D. Cohn

For information, please write:

Steven D. Cohn, Founder
www.WriteItForMe.com
1511 SW Park Avenue – Suite #1103
Portland, OR 97201

Email: service@LifeText25Lessons.com
www.LifeText25Lessons.com

Publishing House: www.InstantPublisher.com

Library of Congress Catalog Card Number: 2006907611
ISBN 1-59872-584-X
ISBN-13: 978-1-59872-584-1
10 9 8 7 6 5 4 3 2

Thank You to...

Heather, my darling wife

Mom, Dad, Dan

Family and lifelong friends
(you can feel who you are)

Well-wishing souls and new friends

Christine Guardiano for opening a new door
Dave Jarecki and Sarah B.H. for editing

Life's many teachers

A WORD TO PARENTS, TEACHERS, and FACILITATORS

This book flowed through my being, waking me at 3 o'clock one recent morning, so I could joyfully record it on paper.

The lessons are intended to enrich the lives of students of all ages (including you). The book is organized into very short "assignments" or exercises: awareness-building activities to be repeated at different times during our lives. Whenever we need such reminding lessons most, this "LifeText" will be here for us.

Certain of the exercises will work well even with children as young as 6. Others will be best understood and first enjoyed a little later on.

The difference between this tool and classical textbooks is: this book encourages a highly *personal* set of experiences, maximizing individual relevancy, and it contains no facts, no formulas, no rules, and no expectations.

As such, students will derive the most benefit from this tool if those in supporting roles refrain from any grading, judgments, feedback (unless solicited by the student) or 'requirements' that the student formally finish or hand in any assignment.

→

The purpose of this book is to *supplement*—not to replace—textbooks and other teaching materials that help students learn. The headings in this book such as "Arithmetic" or "Grammar" or "History" are not meant to suggest any extensive (or even traditional) coverage of the subject matter named. Instead, the headings indicate a special space set aside for creativity, exploration, and self-expression within each discipline.

For some assignments, it could be quite helpful for a facilitator/supportive friend to read the assignment to the student(s), especially for those exercises that suggest closing the eyes.

Users may move at whatever pace is most delightful to them: some will try all of the exercises one-after-the-other, while others will randomly select a single lesson every few weeks or months, repeating the lessons they like most.

Blank pages surround each lesson. Participants are free to enjoy the infinity of these blank pages or to decorate them with words or artwork.

Thank you so much for sharing and for being.

-- *Steven D. Cohn*
Portland, Oregon

Lesson #1:
Being

Assignment:

Find a quiet place. It could be in your home, or in a park, or on your way to school, or in a place that is special to you.

Sit down in that quiet place. It can be for 10 seconds, for 10 minutes, or for as long as you like.

Close your eyes. Focus on the sound of your breathing. Focus on each breath you take in and each breath you breathe out.

There is no right or wrong way to do this. The way you choose to do this is perfect.

Notice how you feel.

Lesson #2:
Nature

Assignment:

Right now, imagine something in nature that interests you or that makes you feel calm. A few examples are: a bird, a tree, a squirrel, an insect, a cloud, a flower, the moon, sand, soil, a river, rain, the blue sky, the wind, a leaf, a rock, a snowflake, or anything else in nature that fills your imagination with excitement, love, or calmness.

The next time you encounter this thing in nature that you just imagined, look at it more closely than you have ever looked at it before. Listen to it. Notice everything you can about it.

Use all of your senses to enjoy it.

After this experience, ask yourself: have you discovered anything new about it… or about yourself?

Lesson #3:
Giving

Assignment:

Imagine someone who needs something.
It could be someone you love; it could be
someone you don't like; or it could be
someone you've never met before.

Imagine yourself giving this person the thing
that he or she needs most.

Imagine that the person doesn't say "thank
you," but that the person is smiling inside
after you give her or him the thing that he or
she needs most.

How do you feel when you think about that?

Lesson #4:
Receiving

Assignment:

Imagine that you feel like something is missing inside you or around you, something that would make you feel happier. It could be an object or it could be something like a hug.

Imagine—doing your best to picture every detail with all your heart—that you are <u>now</u> *receiving* the thing that has been missing.

Keep imagining this for a few minutes.

Imagine that you have everything you need.

How do you feel inside when you think about receiving with all of your heart?

Lesson #5:
Passion

Assignment:

Spend at least 15 minutes every day this week doing something that you love doing more than anything else in life.

If you can't do that thing for whatever reason, spend 15 minutes every day imagining doing it—try to *feel* every detail of doing that thing you love doing more than anything else in life.

If you are not sure what you love doing most, pick *any*thing you enjoy doing, or pick one of the other exercises in this book and do the one that sounds or feels the most interesting to you.

[Doing this assignment as an adult can help you remember—and prioritize—what you really *love*, what makes you 'tick,' and what makes you feel most alive! Enjoy! Live!]

Lesson #6:
Connecting with Beauty

Assignment:

Think about a color you really like. Right now, find something near you that is the color you've chosen. Look at it closely. Imagine you are breathing in the color you like so much.

Now think about a color that you really don't like very much. Find something near you right now that is this color. Look at it closely. Even though you don't like that color, find something else about the colored object that makes you feel good. It could be the texture, the shape, the material it's made from, the sound it makes, the way it tastes, or the way it smells. Pay close attention to all of the good things about the object.

Notice that every object has many dimensions.

Lesson #7:
Music

Assignment:

Spend 15 minutes this week listening to music you love.

Spend 15 minutes this week listening to music loved by *someone who is close to you* (whether you like this music or not).

Spend 15 minutes this week listening to music you have never heard before.

How do you feel when you do each of these?

Did you learn anything about yourself?

Did you discover anything about music or about someone else?

Lesson #8:
Nourishment

Assignment:

Eat a food this week that you love more than anything. When you are eating it, eat very slowly and pay close attention to how it tastes and feels in your mouth.

(If you are not able to eat this food, imagine very clearly what this food would taste like as you are eating it. What would it feel like on your tongue?)

Eat a food this week that *someone else* you know loves (whether you love that food or not).

Eat a food this week that you have never tried before.

Did you discover anything?

Lesson #9:
Scent

Assignment:

Imagine something in nature that has a noticeably good aroma, scent, or smell.

The next time you encounter this scent or smell in real life, stop for a long moment to breathe it in deeply. Think of how this smell makes you feel. Does it make you think of anything? [Does it bring back a memory?]

If you breathe in the smell even more deeply, how does it make you feel?

If you close your eyes and breathe in the smell, can you still 'see' the object?

Can you 'smell' music or the color blue?

Lesson #10: Gratitude

Assignment:

Write down or make a video or voice recording of things for which you are thankful.

Look at or listen to your list.

Add things whenever you would like to.

[If you ever feel *sad*, reviewing your list can really help. Re-visiting your list when you are happy can feel great too!]

Lesson #11:
Fear

Assignment:

Write down or make a video or voice recording of things that make you scared.

Ask yourself: *why* am I afraid of each thing?

If you are not sure why you are afraid of a particular thing, ask yourself, "Well, what would happen if I were to *experience* this thing I fear?"

Okay. Now, imagine—doing your best to picture as many details as you can—each of these frightening things right in front of you (or happening to you)—but also imagine yourself being a real-life *superhero* or super-human, feeling remarkably calm and loving and peaceful even in the presence of the things you fear. Now imagine filling each thing you fear with LOVE... and that each floats away gently, like a helium balloon.

Lesson #12:
History

Assignment:

Go to a place you find to be very peaceful.
Sit down.

Think about something that happened a while
ago that makes you feel bad or sad. Think about
the details of this event.

Now, very slowly: shift your <u>attention</u> to
everything around you where you are sitting.
Spend some time really looking. Notice the
detail of everything you see, hear, smell, touch
(or even taste). Take in three deep breaths.

Notice that the past is not as real or as solid as
everything all around you, nor is it as real as the
air inside your lungs in *this* moment, right now.

Know that you can do this anytime: You can
focus on *now*, and everything else disappears.

Lesson #13:
Future

Assignment:

Imagine something you would like to happen soon.

No dream is too big or small. Envision *all* the details.

Think about how you will *feel* when your dream happens. Imagine that it is happening <u>right now</u>.

When you are finished imagining all of the details, take a deep breath and let the details of your dream float away freely… with a smile.

Releasing your dream to sail out into the Universe is like sending a powerful message in a bottle across the sea or like planting a beautiful seed in a garden.

Some day, even quite soon, amazing things will happen! They may even happen at a time that you don't expect or in a way that is very *different* from what you imagined.

If you give your dream *freedom* to unfold according to Nature's rhythm and time schedule (which may feel different from yours), you may receive even *bigger* wonders! *Your dream* and this process set everything in motion!

Lesson #14:
Arithmetic

Assignment:

Start by taking one long, deep breath in. Gently breathe out. *Add* another deep breath in. Breathe out. *Add* a third deep breath in. Breathe out.

Notice how powerful three deep breaths can be. What number of deep breaths makes <u>you</u> feel the best?

Notice that you don't need a calculator, a pencil, paper, computer, or another person to practice this kind of human math.

You are all that you need.

Lesson #15:
Earth Science

Assignment:

Watch and listen to waves of the sea on a calm day.

You can do this in-person at the shore (if you live near a beach) or you can rent, borrow, or download a video or audio recording that features the repetition of these natural waves.

Watch or listen to the waves for about 15 minutes.

Now take a deep breath. Notice your own breathing. Notice that, like the sea, you have a natural rhythm of waves that you take with you wherever you go. Inhale, exhale. You have the calmness of the ocean's waves inside you.

Imagine that *all* things in life could follow a wave-like pattern: we are awake; we are asleep; we are happy sometimes; we are sad sometimes; we are hungry; we are full; it is day; it is night; it is hot outside; it is cold outside.

Waves are the balance of nature.

Lesson #16: Intuition

Assignment:

Think about a time when people you know have told you one thing, but deep down inside you *knew* something else to be true.

Think about a time when you just *knew* it was going to rain and it did or you *just knew* <u>deep down</u> that a certain subject would be interesting to you, even before you learned much about it.

Think for a moment: has anyone ever told you that you "should" do this or you "should" do that, but deep down inside, you know with every part of your being that *your* special path is to do something else?… something different from what people are telling you that you "should" do?

Think about the *knowing* you have deep inside that doesn't come from books or teachers or parents or friends. This knowing can be called '**intuition**,' and when it 'speaks' loudly to you and you listen, it can be your own personal treasure map to a life filled with learning and experiences.

Lesson #17:
Pain

Assignment:

Have you ever accidentally hurt yourself? Do you remember how awful it felt to be in pain?

Do you also remember how you healed from the pain eventually? How it no longer hurt anymore?

Do you remember how, during the time it hurt the most, it was *almost impossible* to imagine how it would feel when the pain was gone or how you would get to the time and place when the pain would be gone?

Whenever you experience pain, if you remember right away that the pain will soon end, just as the waves in the ocean come and go, then you will begin feeling better very quickly. Just by remembering that everything is temporary, you will speed up your healing. It might even hurt less.

If your healthy self *now* could talk to your hurt self in the past (or in the future)… what would you tell yourself to make you feel better?

Lesson #18:
Physical Education

Assignment:

Stretch. Enjoy stretching.

Lesson #19:
Biology, Chemistry,
Something Else?

Assignment:

Think (and feel) about these questions:

1. What makes you different from the people around you? What makes you one-of-a-kind?

2. What makes you similar to other creatures (including people) on Earth?

3. What do you have in common with an ant?

4. What do you have in common with a tree?

5. What do you have in common with a mountain? A river? A cloud? A *thought*?

6. What part of you is the 'real' you?

Lesson #20:
Physics

Assignment:

Go to a safe place.

Jump as high as you can. Notice that you come down.

This is *underline*experiencing*underline* physics or 'physical law' on Earth.

Lesson #21:
Meta-physics

Assignment:

Examine where you are right now. Look all around you. See, hear, smell, and touch everything around you. Put your feet on the ground. Know deeply where you are. Feel it.

Now close your eyes: imagine clearly that you are on top of a windy mountaintop. Imagine the wind blowing through your hair. Feel the cold snow in your socks and the cold damp inside your boots. Hear the whistling of the wind. See the bright sunshine reflecting off the white snow and green trees. Smell the crisp pine needles that you passed on the way up the mountain. Breathe in the cold, crisp mountain air. Hear the crunching ice beneath your boots.

You are on the mountaintop. Yet you are here. You are in two places at once.

Meta-physics allows people or things to be in more than one place at a time.

Lesson #22:
Quantum Physics

Assignment:

Go outside. Watch any bird flying or any tree
standing.

When you observe—when you just look at
something or someone—it *changes* the thing or
person that you are seeing.

Sometimes, the changes in the person or thing with
which we interact are so small, we can't notice the
difference. Other times, the changes are big.
If you look at it with **Love**, the changes can often be
marvelous!

The time you spent looking at the bird or the tree has
made it (and you) even more beautiful because
you've **realized your connection** with it. You've
exchanged energy (sometimes called "Love") with
it. Just by <u>observing</u> anything outside of ourselves,
we *interact* with it. Offering our attention to something changes it and us. Quantum physics suggests
that we are all *connected*: everything that we see.

So, what *you* focus on (and love) matters…

…not just to you, but to the world.

Lesson #23:
Grammar

Assignment:

Express yourself freely.

Write one word, a paragraph, a page, or a whole book. Whatever you choose is perfect!

Choose any topic you want: real or imaginary.

Don't worry what anyone else thinks. Don't worry about making any 'mistakes'—there is no such thing as a mistake when you are creating.

Don't worry about spelling or punctuation or capitalization or anything except for what makes you excited about writing what you are writing.

You may choose to share the writing with anyone you want or with no one. You may hand in what you wrote or keep it to yourself.

It is all okay. It's better than okay. It's great.

Lesson #24:
Sharing

Assignment:

Share something with someone today.

Lesson #25:
Listening

Assignment:

Tell someone that you would like to practice your listening skills.

This is not the same as practicing your memory skills—you will not be tested on what you remember.

Have someone tell you something important to him or her.

Listen to what the person is saying with all of your heart.

As the person is talking, keep listening to the person's words as well as the *feeling* behind his or her words.

When the person is done talking, you may wish to tell the person that you have heard what he or she has said. If you feel like it, you may thank the person for sharing what he or she has shared.

Nothing more is required. Listening is not the same as responding, judging, helping, or doing. Listening itself is a gift you can give someone.

Share your experiences
(only *if* you'd like to)…

I would love to hear about your experiences
with this book… any you'd like to share.
What did you learn from your favorite lessons?

What would you like to see in the *next* book?

To tell me and/or to order and receive
additional copies of this book:

please visit
www.LifeText25Lessons.com

You may also write to:

Steven D. Cohn, Founder
www.WriteItForMe.com
1511 SW Park Avenue – Suite #1103
Portland, OR 97201

steve@LifeText25Lessons.com

Many thanks and much gratitude.

–Steve

B
The **E**nd
    g
    i
    n
     n
     i
      n
      g